ZC HORSES
CHICK
THE MOM!

Diane W. Keaster

illustrated by Denise McRea

ISBN 0-9721496-2-7

Printed in U.S.A.

ZC HORSES
CHICK
THE MOM!

To my sons for helping me to see the world and a horse through a child's eye.

ZC HORSES
SERIES

Be part of them all!

Chick - The Beginning!

Chick - The Saddle Horse!

Chick - The Mom!

Luke - The First!

And Many More!

ZC HORSES
CHICK
THE MOM!

1

RANCH JOBS

Being raised on a ranch is a privilege. Ranch life is a treasure chest full of memories and experiences. No matter how old you get, those times remain in your heart and mind.

One treasure of ranch life was

working closely with my family. Growing up with three older brothers can be quite a challenge! We always had exciting jobs to do. We always had fun.

One job was to feed cows in the winter. Feeding time was always frigid. The brisk, arctic wind whipped the fluffy snow into a funnel. At times, the snow pelted your face like tiny arrows.

Quite often when feeding, I drove the pickup. I even drove before my legs were long enough to reach the floor. My father put the truck in low gear. That way, the truck crawled like a snail while I turned the steering wheel with my tiny hands. I had to stick my chin high in the air to be able to see. Our dog Pete sat beside me. The smell of crisp hay seeped into the truck.

While I maneuvered the truck, my father or brothers would feed. They looked like giants standing on a trailer hooked onto the truck. The trailer followed the truck like the tail of a snake. It bounced off the ground when going over the frozen mounds of dirt. Gophers, small rodents, left those mounds from their digging in the summer. As the truck crept, the frozen ground under it creaked. Once the truck and trailer were moving, my father or brothers pushed bunches of the stiff hay onto the ground. "Swoosh" the hay sounded as the trailer left behind a trail of green.

Black, red, yellow and white cows came at a high lope to eat their dinner. Once to the green 'river', the cows' heads went down. They then looked up with hay hanging out their mouths. They watched us fade away, chomping on their green meal.

In the summer, we had a different job. We made that delicious hay to feed the cows. This involved a lot of steps. First, wild grass or alfalfa (a plant of the pea family) had to be cut. Either my father or one of my brothers would drive the tractor, or swather, and do the cutting. The swather left the cuttings in a row, or windrow, to dry in the scorching summer sun. The dried ribbons of hay were now put into a baler. The baler spit out either little square bales or large round bales. Pete always trotted behind. As if counting the bales, he watched them drop to the ground.

Before I had a job driving the tractor, I had to topple over the small square bales with my feet. The plant stalks left on the ground were stiff. They poked my legs as I walked. The smell of fresh hay surrounded me. Pete watched intently as I pushed over the bales. Small mice scurried from under the bales. Sometimes, though, I had to jump back quickly. Quite often, a rattlesnake awaited. Its eerie rattle filled the air before I saw the treacherous reptile. Pete lept back, too.

Once the bales dotted the fields, they had to be picked. They were very heavy, so this was a hard job. The heat of a bright summer day never helped. Small streams slithered through many of the fields. It was nice to stop for a moment and jump into their cool waters. Bales rested in large haystacks until winter-feeding time.

Fall and spring brought the best job of all. That was to move the cows from pasture to pasture. In the spring, we moved the cows with their little babies, or calves. Calves cried out and jumped and bucked as we went.

Spring was such a pretty time. Flowers and plants were beginning to awaken from their winter sleep. The air smelled so fresh and carried scents of each flower. The sky always looked so blue. Filling the countryside were babies of all sorts. My favorite was the baby horse, or foal.

Fall cattle drives involved bringing the cows closer to home. The trees showed off their brilliant orange, red and yellow leaves. Nearby mountains already wore their clean, white caps. The small creeks, or streams, were bordered with paper-thin ice. The crisp air stung your face. Sometimes we even rode in moist snow. Wild geese and ducks scolded us with their "Honk, Honk" or "Quack, Quack" as they flew overhead in their 'V'.

Moving cows involved riding my horse. I was always happiest riding my horse. Through the years, I rode many different horses. Eagle was palomino, or yellow. Smoky was gray and got whiter the older he got. Bobby Sox was red with a pretty flaxen mane and tail. A flaxen tail is red with white hairs scattered through it. She also had four white stockings. This means the white on her legs went from her hoof, or foot, way up her leg. Sarge was bay, being red with a black mane and tail.

Even though I loved all the horses I rode, Chick was my pride and joy. We always had so many wonderful rides together. Whether we were moving cows or riding for fun, they were always special times. Because I enjoyed riding her so, I had a tough decision to make. One job a horse has on a ranch is to work cows. Another job is to raise babies, or foals. The reason I bought her was to ride her for a while, then get some babies from her.

The time came for Chick to become a 'Mom' instead of a 'Saddle Horse'!

2

LUKE - THE FIRST

Deciding Chick should become a mom was very hard. It was exciting though. We had become so close during our rides.

I always enjoyed seeing the newborn foals in the spring. It was fun to see if they were boys (colts) or girls (fillies). It was also fun to see their color when they 'dropped', or were born.

My brother owned a beautiful stallion. His name was 'Shane's Print'. He was a deep chestnut, or dark red. Printer, as we called him, was very gentle, too. His body was very muscular. What an ideal father he would be! He lived by the creek close to the house. Both he and Chick were friends with the geese. They all shared the same area.

I was still not sure who the father of Chick's first foal should be. I went out to the corral. Printer stood at the back. It was springtime. The smell of new grass took my breath away. Leaves were starting to show on the trees. Printer shot a glance at me. Then he came walking slowly and smoothly up to me. He put his head down so I could pet him. That was it! Printer was to be the father.

Chick was born on April 25. It was right around that same time that she was to foal, or have her baby. I had to wait just over eleven months for Chick to foal. That time lasted forever! I did not ride Chick during those months. I was riding Radar. He was a blue roan. That meant he had black and white hairs mixed throughout his body. This made him appear blue. I wanted Chick to be able to relax and be careful so as not to hurt the baby.

During the long wait for the baby, I pampered Chick. I gave her special food and brushed her soft, golden coat. With every month that passed, Chick got heavier with her baby. When I put my head against her warm stomach, I heard many interesting noises. Sometimes, too, when I put my hand on her tummy, I felt the baby kick! Everyday I studied Chick and I studied Printer. It was so fun trying to picture this wonderful first foal. Would it be chestnut? Would it be palomino? Would it be a colt? Would it be a filly? Would it have white socks? Would it have white on its face? How big would it be? There were so many questions to be answered!

The time for the foal to drop drew near. Every night before I went to bed, I went outside and talked to Chick. Several times during the night, I went outside to check on her. The stars glittered in the dark sky. Sometimes, the Northern Lights, or Aurora Borealis, shot their magnificent colors through the sky. When this happened, I sat with Chick for some time and watched in amazement. She always placed her soft head beside me. She studied me with her gentle, brown eyes. I checked on Chick many times. I was beginning to wonder if she really was going to foal!

Knowing Chick was to foal around April 25, I was very concerned on April 24. That night, I woke up during the night many times to check Chick. Chick acted normal every time I went out. In the morning, I felt my mother nudging me. When I looked up at her, she said, "I have to tell you...", and she paused. My heart sunk I was so scared. I knew something bad happened. Then she continued, "Chick had her baby, but it won't get up."

I sprung out of bed and threw on my clothes. What had happened?! Pete followed as I rushed to the corral. Frost rested upon the fence. When I got out to Chick's pen, the foal was still flat on the ground. Chick was up with her nose gently nudging the foal. I was close to crying. Pete sat at the edge of the corral with his head hanging. As I got closer, Chick's concerned eyes caught mine. A subtle nicker slipped from her sad lips. A faint nicker flowed from the foal. I eased up to the baby. Then with one leap, it was up! Chick nickered again, but louder this time. The baby joyfully nickered back. It nuzzled its mom with its tiny nose. Its slender legs were spread out and wobbling.

I was elated! The foal was healthy and fine. Although it was still wet from just being born, I could see the baby was a beautiful, golden palomino. Just like its mom. It had its mom's blaze, or white down its face. I saw right away it was a colt.

Immediately I tagged him with the name 'Luke'.

To help a horse like people, they need to be around you as soon as they are born. I got next to Luke. I put one arm around his front and the other arm around his rear. He jumped a little while I held him. Then he settled down. Talking softly to him I scratched his tender ears. Calmly he looked at me with his big, brown eyes. They were framed by soft, white eyelashes. I knew right away we were going to get along great. We shared many scary times when he got older.

Luke right away nursed on his mom, or drank her milk. A feeling of joy overwhelmed me while

I watched them. I left mother and child alone to get to know each other.

All that waiting was worth it. I knew it was going to be around April 25. It was not until after I went into the house that I realized that Luke was born on the same day as Chick.

Handling Luke did not prepare me for Chick's next baby!

3

BARBIE - THE BEST

Luke turned out to be a wonderful horse. Having Printer as his father and Chick as his mother was a good choice. I decided to have a different father, though, for Chick's next foal.

After looking, I found a beautiful

gray stallion. He was what is called a 'speckle gray'. That means, he was gray with red flecks through his coat of hair. He had been used as a cutting horse in contests. He also ran races. His disposition, or personality, too, was very gentle. His name was 'Dan's Bar'. I called him 'Dan'. The one drawback about Dan being the father was that the owners wanted to sell him. Since he was such a fabulous stallion, I made the purchase. He was the father to Chick's next three foals.

Again, Chick's foaling date was around April 25. Those eleven months of waiting always seemed so long. Chick spent those months in a nice, green pasture with good grass. Through the pasture ran a sparkling, clear creek with brush alongside it.

Like with Luke, I was very nervous when April came. Chick was now in a grassy pen beside the barn. I checked her all through the night for weeks. She always acted like nothing was happening. She was heavier with every passing day.

I checked Chick early one spring morning and nothing. About half an hour later, there was a knock on the door. As I opened it, the neighbor stood, wearing a big smile. He never said a word. He just pointed over to the barn. There stood Chick. Wobbling beside her was a gorgeous, dark-red baby! I rushed to them. Chick looked at me with a sparkle in her eye. Once again she fooled me! The foal was healthy and perfectly built. It was a filly. Although she was a dark red, there were a few gray hairs through her, like her father. This meant she would turn gray. A gray horse is always dark colored, either black, brown or red, when they are born. The older they get, the lighter they turn. They will be completely white when they get real old, like Smokey. Their mane and tail may stay darker.

This filly also had the same blaze on her face as her mom. She also wore two pretty, white socks on her back legs.

This filly was so beautiful I had to think of a special name for her. Since I had always loved playing with Barbie Dolls, I named her Barbie. I wanted her full name to be 'Bar B Dial'. It ended up being 'Super Bar Dial'.

Right away I put my arms around Barbie, like I did with Luke. While Luke jumped a little, Barbie bucked right in my arms. She had me bouncing up and down like a rubber ball. I thought she would never stop! No matter how softly I talked to her, she kept it up. It took a long time for her to quit.

When Barbie was a day old, I put a pretty, little blue halter on her. She did not like that. She tried to pull away from me. She jumped. She bucked. She ran. It was a struggle, but finally I could lead her. Although she had a lot of spunk, I knew she would be one that would always be close to me. There was something very special about her. We had many wonderful and special times together as she aged.

Handling Barbie made me even more anxious to see Chick's next foal. I felt I knew for sure the date it would drop. Like Luke and Chick, Barbie was also born on April 25.

Chick's next foal was quite a surprise!

4

GOLDIE - THE WISE

Another eleven months now had to pass. Again there were so many questions to be answered. What color was the foal to be? Would it be a filly or colt? What markings, or white areas, would the foal wear? I figured since Barbie was a gray, the color of the new foal would be gray, like their father. It was so exciting to think Barbie would have a little brother or sister. Since Barbie was a filly, I thought the next foal might be a colt. I could not wait to find out!

Chick spent the next eleven months in a nice, lush pasture. It was right next to the house. Part of the pasture was the side of the coulee, a small valley. There was a small spring half way up. A spring is where water comes out of the ground. My brothers and I used to sled down this hill in the winter. At the back part of the pasture was a small pond. I would take an inner tube up to it. Slimy fish swam around me while I floated.

Again, when April finally arrived, I checked on Chick continuously. Again, she always acted like nothing was happening. I knew something was happening. She got heavier every day.

On April 24, I knew I had to watch Chick carefully. She and her first two foals were born on April 25. All through the night, I went out to the pasture to see if Chick showed any signs of foaling. It was a very dark night. The moon was not shining. The twinkling stars were my only light. Once I found Chick, there were no signs. She only stood quietly, glancing at me with her sleepy eyes. Maybe this foal was not going to be born on the same day.

The next morning, as soon as I got out of bed, I checked on Chick. What a surprise! There, standing beside her with sturdy legs, was a beautiful, palomino filly! Since she had the same golden color as her mom, I called her 'Goldie'. Her real name was to be 'Golden Bar Dial'.

Goldie wore the same white blaze as her mother. Her mane and tail were silky white. Her father's (Dan's) looks did not show up in her at all.

As I approached, they stood completely still. Chick looked so proud! Pete sat back, wagging his tail. I put my arms around Goldie, like I did the other two. She did not jump or fight at all. I scratched her ears and whispered. She stood quietly. It was as if she understood each word I said.

The next day, I put on Goldie the tiny blue halter. It did not bother

her a bit. When I went to lead her along, she followed. There was no fighting or bucking or pulling or jumping. She was so smart! Whatever I asked of her, she did. The biggest surprise was when I started riding her.

Once again, on April 25, Chick gave me a fantastic baby. I could not believe my eyes when she gave me the next!

5

CHICKADEE - THE TRAVELER

I tried not to think about the next foal for the following eleven months. Chick spent her time in a comfortable pasture. There was plenty of room to run. There was plenty of good feed and water. She could overlook the Belt Valley, near where we lived. At the bottom, was Belt Creek. It was a small river lined with large, billowing trees. The quaint town of Belt was almost hidden by the leafy arms of the green giants. Across the valley, Chick could see the thimble-shaped Belt Butte towering into the deep, blue sky. The butte showed off its permanent, rock belt. A continual breeze flowed through Chick's mane and tail.

Chick came home as her foaling date neared. I calculated she would drop her foal on April 25. I watched her carefully every day, anyway. I checked her often through the night.

On April 24, I could hardly wait for the next day. I had left the house for just a short while. I knew Chick was safe in a pen close to the house. Looking at her as I left, I thought how nice it would be to have a black foal. I knew that would be impossible as Chick was palomino and Dan was gray. Chick looked content, resting against the barn.

Having only been gone for a few minutes, I did not feel the need to check on Chick. It was a warm, sunny spring day. The sun glowed in the blue sky that went on forever. Shooting a glance at her pen, I thought I saw a dark spot beside her. I knew this could not be. I was probably just seeing things since I desired a black foal. Not being able to get the 'black spot' out of my mind, I walked over to the pen.

I could not believe what I saw! Chick proudly trotted around the pen. Beside her trotted the most fabulous black filly. Her head was high in the air like she was a princess! I said to her, "Come here my little chickadee!" She cautiously came to me. From then on I called her 'Chickadee'. Her real name was 'Chickadee Bar Dial'.

I was surprised Chickadee was black since her mom was palomino and dad was gray. I then remembered, her grandmother, Chick's mom, was as black as coal. I studied Chickadee's soft, furry coat. She did have just a few flecks of gray frosting the black. Chickadee only had a small spot of white, called a star, between her eyes. Her legs were totally black.

Like Barbie, Chickadee put up a fight when I gathered her in my arms. She hopped up and down like a yo-yo. With the halter fastened, she did not want to lead, either. It was quite a struggle convincing her to follow.

There was one thing that was very different about Chickadee. Her walk. When she and her mom were walking side by side, Chickadee passed her mom. Her little head swung like a pendulum

in rhythm with her walk. She was a very fast walker from the day she was born. Riding her was quite an experience.

Dan, the father of Chickadee, Barbie and Goldie, was very old. He did not sire, or father, any more foals. I felt very fortunate to get from him these fine babies. I think of him whenever I look at his off-spring.

Now came the adopted brother!

6

THE BEST MOM

Spring is a spectacular time of year. Many wonderful things take place. The white carpet of snow gradually melts into the ground. Moisture eventually seeps into nearby creeks and rivers. Raging currents of fresh water grow larger with every warm day. Life and beauty is put back into dormant flowers. The time of rest for the green vegetation comes to an end. Lean, lifeless trees start wearing their leafy, spring coat. The rolling countryside comes alive with color. Hills are patterned with a lush, green blanket decorated with dots of purple, pink, yellow, red and blue.

The clear blue sky houses the radiant sun. Light showers invite the plants, trees and flowers for a refreshing drink. Soft breezes dance with robust trees.

The best part of spring, though, has to be the beginning of lives. All types of babies are born. During springtime, you see baby pigs, cows, horses, elk, deer, and rabbits. You can play with tiny, fluffy kittens.   Frolic with ram-bunctious puppies.   Marvel at floating baby ducks and geese. The list of these precious, delicate gifts goes on and on.

There is a special bond between a mother and her baby. It does not matter if you are a person or an animal.   Chick had that special bond with all of her foals. When an animal or person is a mother, they seem to care about all young-sters. It does not matter whether they are their own. Chick had this instinct.

Chickadee was just a few days old. She and Chick were enjoying the new, spring grass. They were pas-tured with a few cows and calves.

A slight breeze put towering trees in motion. Their leaves shivered on the branches. Chick seemed to not notice Chickadee running, bucking and kicking in a circle around her. Chick kept her head to the ground, enjoying the sweet, fresh meal.

Watching them with a warm glow inside me, I noticed something beside Chick. I knew it was not the frisky Chickadee. She continued to romp around her mom. I decided I had better walk out to see. The closer I got, the more amazed I was. I could not believe my eyes. There beside Chick, nursing on her, or drinking milk from her, was a little black and white calf, or baby cow. The calf did not care that this was not her mother. Chick did not care that it was not her baby. Chickadee only cared about zipping here and there.

This showed the love a mother holds in her heart. That motherly love will set everything else aside to provide care. It proved that a mother is happy to be just that. A mother to someone or something. Every so often, Chick glanced at the baby calf. She never budged. She never dreamed of hurting it. She continued to be a mother!

Unlike the calf, Chick's next foal was one you did not want to take your eyes off of!

7

SONNY - THE SPECTACULAR

The father of Chick's next foal was a sorrel. That is a red colored horse. I was very anxious to see the color of this foal. I had to wait those agonizing eleven months again, though.

I knew this foal would be unique. None of Chick's foals had ever had a sorrel as a father. The other stallions had been chestnut and gray. Since Chick's mother was black, there could always be the chance of the foal being black. Chick's father was sorrel. I felt there was a good chance for this foal to be sorrel. This foal's father would be sorrel and mother, Chick, was a golden palomino. She already had two palomino foals. After pondering these things, I decided for sure the foal would be a sorrel. Now all I had to do was wait to see!

The time had come for Chick to foal. Once again, Chick would not allow me to see her foal drop. She always fooled me. I would think she was not yet going to foal. In a couple of hours, her baby stood beside her.

Like before, I checked Chick all through the night. Nothing. Then, in the morning, Chick's new filly was standing strong next to her.

This foal was gorgeous. She was a beautiful, light-colored palomino. She had a blaze on her face, just like her mom's. Her body was built elegantly. She held her head like she was a queen. Her most appealing attribute was her mane and tail. They were a clean, bright white. Nothing could be whiter. To the touch, they were like silk. A horse's mane and tail are thick. It is tough to get a brush through them. A light comb was all that was needed to glide through the mane and tail of this foal.

As the foal stood next to her mom, the sun peaked out from behind a fluffy cloud. Rays of sunshine kissed Chick and her new little girl. This made the filly look all the more beautiful. I then decided to call her 'Sonny'.

Sonny always was very kind and friendly. She loved people. The look in her eyes was extremely soft and gentle. She was very cooperative when I first held her. She followed along behind me like a puppy when I first put the tiny halter on her petite head. That, I guess, is why I was surprised when I first rode her!

As a baby, Chick's next foal kept me on my toes!

8

ONIE - THE ROANIE

Printer had been gone for some time. My brother had a new stallion. He was a beautiful, majestic red roan. A red roan's coat has red and white hairs through it. His mane and tail were red. This stallion's name was Tio Jose'. We called him Jose'. I felt he and Chick would have a wonderful foal together.

During these eleven months, Chick rested in a green pasture on a sloping hillside. A mountain above her reached to the sky. Elk, a type of large deer, liked to rest there. They even had their babies close. One of her companions was a black and white goat. His name was Herman. He never left her side. Herman had horns about eight inches long that tilted to one side. When I whistled for Chick, Herman came running right behind her. It was quite a sight watching them come off the hill at a high lope! Herman even trotted along when we went for rides.

Time finally neared for Chick to foal. April 25 had come and gone. I was getting very nervous. It was already three weeks past the eleven months. This could mean something was wrong with the foal.

All through each night I checked on Chick. It was a very rainy month. One night carried a treacherous rainstorm. The wind threw sheets of cold, pounding rain against me. I was soaked after checking on Chick. She held her head low to keep the water pellets from slapping her. The hillside was very slick. The wall of rain cut off the beam from my flashlight. Chick could get into the large barn, but she did not want that. An owl sat at the top inviting her with his, "Whoo, Whoo". She still would not come in out of the rain.

In the morning, I immediately ran to Chick. She was as far up the hill as she could get. The fence blocked her from going farther. Fluffy white clouds were setting low on the top of the mountain. The crisp air smelled fresh from the night's washing. There, beside her, was the most outstanding, magnificent strawberry roan colt. A strawberry roan is a very light, frosted red roan. He had a very small star on his forehead. He was absolutely brilliant.

There was no doubt in my mind what I would call him. Quite often when people see a roan horse, they say it is a "roanie". He was one of the prettiest "roanies" I had ever seen. I knew I would call him 'Onie'. His full name was 'Go Dial Charge Onie'.

As I got close to Chick and Onie, he nickered softly. His mom put her nose down to him to assure him he was fine. I went to gather him in my arms, but he did not want that. It took a bit of trying, but finally I caught him. He put up a big fight. He not only bucked, jumped and pulled. He also kicked and struck. He had quite a temper!

Onie reacted the same when I put on his new little halter. He fought and fought and fought. He did not want me to lead him at all! He put up a fight for a long time then finally settled into the routine. Riding him was a different story.

I did not think Chick could give me any foal prettier than Onie.

What she gave me next, though, was unbelievable!

9

TAWNY - THE BEAUTY

The father to Chick's next baby was easy to choose. I once bought a wonderful gelding. A gelding is a male horse that cannot be a father. This gelding was very smooth to ride. He was also gentle, smart and loved to work cows. When chasing cows, he pinned his ears back and stayed right on their tail. He was also very good looking. Right then I knew I wanted a horse like him.

To get a horse like him, I would have to have either his brother or sister. So his father was to be the father of Chick's next foal. That stallion's name was 'My Leroy Brown'. He was a very handsome, dark-brown stallion. Like Dan, he had been in 'cow-cutting' contests. Also like Dan, he had been a racehorse.

Those eleven months were almost unbearable. I felt this would be Chick's best foal. I had already planned on it becoming my main saddle horse.

Chick's pasture during these eleven months had a creek running through it. There was always the fear of her foaling too close to the creek. Since a foal's legs are wobbly at first, they cannot stand well. Sometimes they even fall. If the foal fell into the cold water, it would not be able to get out.

When the time neared for Chick to foal, I was overly nervous. I knew this was going to be a spectacular foal. On the way to see Chick, I decided I had better start checking on her throughout the night. This was especially necessary with that terrifying creek.

Once again Chick fooled me. Standing proudly beside her was a beautiful, golden palomino filly. She had the same white blaze, mane and tail as her mom. She was identical to Chick! I did not even have the chance to check on Chick throughout the night!

I had once read a book about a golden-colored dog. Its name was 'Tawny'. I had never forgotten that name. That was it. I named her 'Tawny'. Her full name was 'Leroy's Tawny Dial'.

Tawny was very easy to handle. She did not mind at all that I held her. There was no fight in her. When I put the little halter on her head, she just stood. When I wanted to lead her away, she followed like my shadow. She was already like her half-brother I had ridden.

Smart and gentle and extremely good-looking.

Tawny was very stunning. I knew after being around her that I made the right choice in wanting her to be my new saddle horse. My dreams, though, were crushed by tragedy when the time came to ride her.

What a treat she was!

10

THE GIFTS

I viewed each foal as a gift from Chick. Chick was never upset about me being around her babies. She always stayed a friend to me.

Chick was a fantastic mother to each and every one of her foals. Each baby was an actor or actress in its own play. They may have been shy, frisky, ornery or quiet. They each had their own personality. But they were all a part of Chick. They all brought me innumerable joys during my handling of them. Each foal started out as Chick's baby. Each then went on with their own story to tell. Some even having their own babies, their own rides, their own joys, and their own sorrows. I rode all of them and had many enjoyable times.

All of Chick's foals gave me another good reason for being happy our paths had crossed. No horse could be loved as much as Chick. The way Chick loved her children is the way all mothers should show love. The love shown between mother and child is a treasure.

ZC HORSES SERIES

Now that you have met some of Chick's foals, you can read about them! Find out what it was like breaking, training, working with and riding them. Get to know them better and hear their stories. Luke is the first to read about in *"Luke-The First!"*. Go with him through the forest and a treacherous thunderstorm. Learn about his tragic accident.

Be sure to be there to greet him!!
ZC HORSES SERIES #4
Luke - The First!
by Diane W. Keaster

To My Reader:

I was born and raised on a ranch near a little town called Belt, Montana. After receiving my B.S. in Business Education from Montana State University, I taught high school business. I then moved on to other facets of employment.

The whole time, I was team roping and raising, breaking and training horses. The profession I fell into by mistake was trading horses. Throughout my life, I have handled hundreds of horses, all which have a story of their own.

I have two sons, Cole and Augustus, who also rope and have a love for and talent with horses. We ride our horses for enjoyment into mountain lakes, help local ranchers with their cattle, golf, water ski, downhill ski and snowboard, cross-country ski, fish, roller blade, ride bike and laugh together. We have dogs, cats, rabbits, chickens, ducks, geese, fish, and George, the parrot. We live near the beautiful Salmon River at Salmon, Idaho.

My boys loved reading stories about horses and I loved reading the stories to them. That is why I am writing these books. I want to tell the stories of the creatures I love to the children I love.

I thank Jehovah our Creator for giving us such a wonderful, beautiful animal!

What about Chick? She is still enjoying her retirement on my mother's ranch at Belt, visiting with my mom's and brother Gary's horses.

Enjoy the stories!

Order Form
ZC HORSES SERIES

Don't miss out on any part of the lives of Chick and her many babies and friends! Experience all of the rides, joys and sorrows. Don't be left out!

___	Chick-The Beginning! (Spring 2001)	$7.95
___	Chick-The Saddle Horse! (September 2001)	$7.95
___	Chick-The Mom! (April 2002)	$7.95
___	Luke-The First! (September 2002)	$7.95
___	Barbie-The Best! (Oct. 2002)	$7.95
___	Leroy-The Stallion! (September 2003)	$7.95
___	Goldie-The Wise! (March 2004)	$7.95
___	Chickadee-The Traveler! (June 2004)	$7.95
___	Darby-The Cow Dog! (September 2004)	$7.95
___	Sonny-The Spectacular! (November 2004)	$7.95

UPCOMING TITLES

Tawny-The Beauty!   Apple-The Joy!
Onie-The Roanie!   Belle-The Sweetie!
Classy-The Special!   Lily-The Pretty Paint!
Black Jack-The Great !   Slick-TheFriend!

Also read about Cider, Buck, Nellie, Junie, Eagle, Smokey, Sarge, Tex, Radar and many more!

-ZC HORSES SERIES, 8 Hknsn Ln, Salmon, ID 83467
(208) 756-7947
www.zchorses.com
Email: zchorses@hotmail.com

Please send me the books I have checked above. I am enclosing US $___ (please add $2/bk or $4/order to cover shipping and handling). Send check or money order, please. Prices subject to change.

NAME_____

ADDRESS_____

CITY/STATE/ZIP_____

PHONE_____

NOTES AND PICTURES!!!!

NOTES AND PICTURES!!!!

.

NOTES AND PICTURES!!!!

NOTES AND PICTURES!!!!

NOTES AND PICTURES!!!!

NOTES AND PICTURES!!!!

NOTES AND PICTURES!!!!

NOTES AND PICTURES!!!!

NOTES AND PICTURES!!!!

NOTES AND PICTURES!!!!

.

NOTES AND PICTURES!!!!

NOTES AND PICTURES!!!!

NOTES AND PICTURES!!!!

NOTES AND PICTURES!!!!

Made in the USA
San Bernardino, CA
11 July 2015